Manifest

Debbie Viale

SWEETSPIRE LITERATURE
——— MANAGEMENT ———

Table of Contents

The Black Wall

Running through a dark tunnel,
A maze if you will,
Sounds of human cries,
Climbed the window seal,
Grasping for air covered with ash,
Ears ringing in tune with my heart beating,
Smells of disaster and disbelief,
Running through a dark tunnel,
A maze if you will,
Alone with my heart beat,
Against a wall,
I stood still…

At The Door

Please listen to your Mother,
She's been there once before,
Thank God her Dad could be there,
To meet him at the door,
Her Brother came up behind him,
To offer her Dad a hand,
Please don't ask what happened,
Let's just say her Dads a Man,
Please listen to your Mother,
She's been there once before,
Thank God her Dad could be there,
To meet him at the door...

The Cabin

My Grandfather built a cabin,
On the outskirts by the bay,
Strong as the foundation,
He built his wedding day,
Every year a baby,
Filled this home with love,
Blessed by the angels,
Sent from up above,
The barn housed 4 horses,
To plow the land for food,
They shared with their neighbors,
From the porch on Sunday noon,
Sat and told old stories,
Until the setting of the moon,
The cabin is still standing,
On the outskirts by the bay,
And if you want to see it,
I'll take you out that way......

Who Are You

Who are you,
Do you hear my voice,
In the silent void,
Of your traffic jam each day,
Where do you go,
In your lapse of consciousness each night,
Are your dreams parallel to mine,
Or are we one,
Divided in time,
Who are you…

Leo Lion

You drank away our memories,
From tomorrow's yesterday,
You drove our childs history,
A million miles away,
Leo Lion roaring,
Atop the center stage,
I took away your freedom,
Locked you up inside a cage,
Then you got so angry,
You tortured me with rage,
We always seemed to be,
On opposite sides of the page…..

Stars Were Bright

The stars were bright throughout the night,
I thought I saw a U.F.O
But what it was I'll never know,
I see what hides behind your fears,
I wake each morning with your tears.
Feel the waves throughout the stars,
I will dream away all your scars,
I rather see a grown Man,
Break down and cry,
Than to have to hear him tell a lie,
The stars were bright throughout the night,
And what I saw I'll never know,
Until you see the light of day.
I must find another way…

The Game

Your eyes so dark,
Mysterious but wise,
Your action figure frame,
Blind-sided by your knowledge,
And strength that makes you Man
The game you are so good at,
Catch me if you can,
She sent you to the moon,
On a freight train in the rain,
Your passion was the victim,
Of the strength that made you Man,
The game you are so good at,
Catch me if you can…

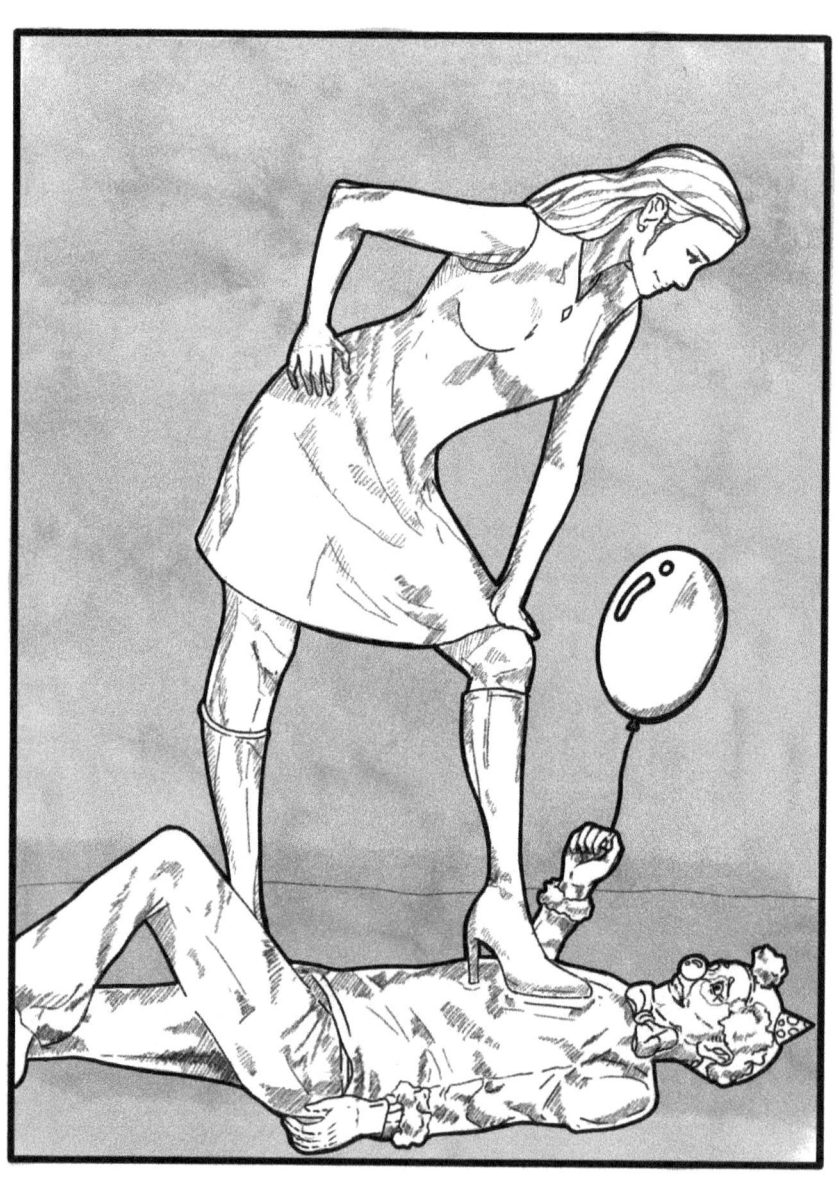

True Colors

You lean on the bottle,
You sneak out the door,
You lie to my face,
I can't wait anymore,
I'm not your Dog,
And I'm not your whore,
I'll punch you in the face,
And I'll settle the score,
Don't cross my trust
Don't break my heart
You showed your true colors,
Right from the start.
Lay down your cards,
Place your bets on the table.
Plant your feet on the ground,
Take a look around,
You think you know this game,
Until she came around,
She will put you to work,

and give you some fame,
You'll spend it all chasing,
The magic in the game,
She's smart at the art
You only have yourself to blame
She'll get a hold of your heart
Then crush it through your veins,
You'll wish you never met her,
But it's the magic in the game,
That will drive you insane,
take a look in the mirror,
That reflection is you,
Stop treating others,
Disrespectful and cruel…

The Heart of Aids

Through all the weathered time we've spent,
You would think we would get a break,
But we don't always get the chance
to follow out our fate,
The time we had was extra precious
It meant a lot to me,
When you were feeling down and out,
And fought to barely breathe,
If I could hold you close to me,
And never let you go,
I would fight all your pain,
And never let it show,
What I feel the most right now,
Are angry tears of love,
But at the same time I hope and pray,
There is a God above,
And if there were then I would say,
Take him now he's yours,
For every girl and boy,
Please help us find a cure,
So if you're tired and weak my love,
I will understand,
This fight was fought,
Through thick and thin,
So until we meet again…

Morning Glory

Morning glory growing tall,
It covered the fence in no time at all
Every year it grows like weeds,
Producing more flowers,
While dropping more seeds,

Opening each morning,
Then closing at night,
Those flowers are magical,
A magnificent sight,
There's no place like Earth,
This planet of Love

As we grow and we live,
Under the bright stars above…

Storm

The storm came through,
In a viscous blast,
We didn't expect it,
It happened so fast,

It tore through our home,
Like nothing I've known,
It ripped off our roof tops,
Like paper being blown,

Now there is silence,
Like nothing you've known,
Just memories of rubbish,
We used to call home…

Upon Your Derriere

*E*ver felt a hand on your shoulder,
When no ones really there,
Ever felt a pin stick,
Upon your derriere,
Ever had an eye twitch,
Or your knee give out a kick,
Ever had your lip start to shiver,
Remember chewing bazooka gum,
Til your jaw fell on the floor,
How about when you rode your bike,
All the way to the store,
Or when you fall off a step,
That wakes you from your sleep,
Ever ran through the house,
And sank your Mother's cake,
Remember breaking in a baseball glove,
Or blowing bubbles in the tub,
Do you remember the very first time,
You ever fell in love…

The Long Way

What if raindrops,
Were sweet like candy,
And fireflies could talk,
What if we had nine lives,
Seven hundred years,
Before we stopped,
A war could last forever,
No one really knows,
Until you face disaster,
And stars burn out at night,
Leaving you with windmills,
Creating vision in your mind,
How we take the long way,
Around the easy things in life,
Or how we chase the moonlight,
Because we're running from the sun…

Gypsy

Gypsy to the highway,
Pilot in the sky,
Sailor out at sea,
Poet on the page,
Blacksmith on the hoof,
Painting on the wall,
Cherry on the pitt,
Leather on the ball,
Hand in the glove,
Stars shine above,
Cover on the book,
Smile on the face,
Picture I just took,
Gypsy's leather face…

The Climb

Climbed your fence,
Splinter in my knee,
Wore a dress,
Shame on me,
Caught you looking,
Through smoked glass,
The glare of wisdom,
From your past,
August night the moon was bright,
Watched you sleeping in the light,
Sunday gather all as one,
Dear God hold his Father's Son...

Rearview Mirror

I had a friend that needed help,
Her husband beat her down,
I knew I couldn't hide her,
So I took her out of town,
Drove for days on the run,
Rearview mirror I checked her Son,
What a mess she made of,
Such a precious life,
The day I made a promise,
Not to become just someone's wife,
Babies screaming,
Laundry spinning,
Phones are ringing twice,
For her too late to listen,
To her Mother's sound advice…

Shiny

Shiny as a diamond
standing out in a crowd.
I caught a glimpse of madness
Hiding behind the shroud,
Thunder pounded from a distance,
As the rain fell on my face,
Your knight and shining armour,
Held the light,
With all its grace,
Shiny as a diamond,
Standing out in a crowd,
I caught a glimpse of madness
Hiding behind the shroud…

Corona and Lime

Did you whisper my name,
When you woke up this morning,
Did you hear me laughing,
From the sky up above,
Your happiness and kindness,
Just fits like a glove,
Sets you apart from the rest,
Your beauty is enchanting,
Makes me want to build a nest,
I can feel your heartbeat
Right next to mine,
We just fit together
Like a corona and lime…

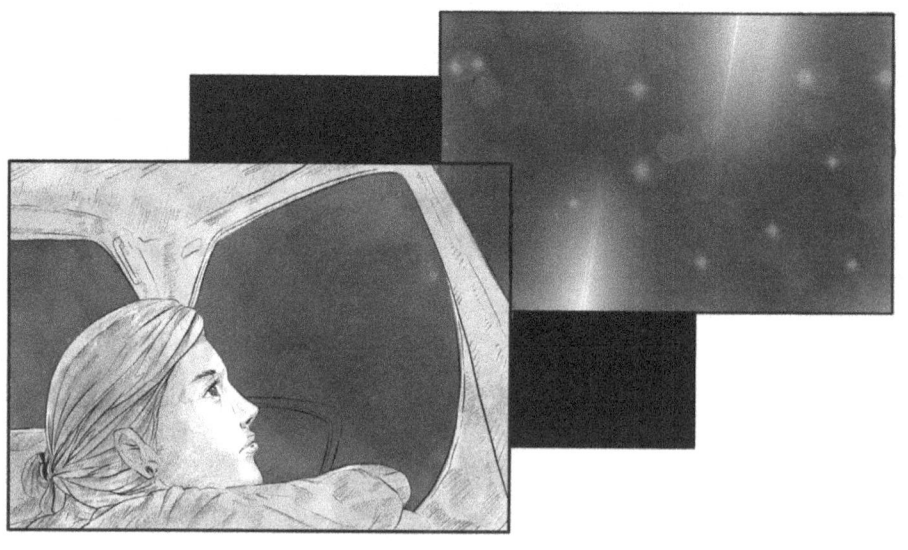

Mystery Glow

A stillness crept under our feet.
As we sat quietly in our chairs,
While a vibration grew near,
Shadows surrounding us,
With a bright red glare,
A mystery glowed in the sky,
Unable to capture a reason why,
We didn't move an inch,
Frozen in time,
Feeling captured by the light,
Something we just couldn't fight,
Just a vision we couldn't explain,
And a restful feeling,
Came across our minds,
Captured by wisdom
And our own peace of mind…

Your Scent

Your soft quiet touch,
Wakes me in the middle of the night,
I don't understand what I feel,
It's magical it has its own light,
I wasn't looking for you,
I wasn't aware you were there,
Your soul waved a scent into the air,
It woke me from a deep sleep,
It turned on a light,
Now I can see you,
You shine through so bright…

Impatient Flames

You seem so far away,
From a distance I can't reach,
I sit alone in my chair,
And twirl my fingers through my hair,
I feel your presence standing near,
I hear your voice in the air,
How much longer will it take,
Impatient flames just can't wait,
Take me by the hand,
And lead the way,
I'm too lost inside my head,
To reach out to you,
How much longer will it take,
Impatient flames just can't wait...

Honesty

Be honest with me,
And I'll be honest with you,
I leave my games at the casino,
At the end of the night I'm through,
Are you afraid of the truth,
Afraid it will hurt me,
Don't fall victim to my darkness,
I can't be hurt anymore,
I thought you could find me,
When you sat down beside me,
Are you here to fix me,
Or am I here to fix you,
Be honest with me,
And I'll be honest with you,
I leave my games at the casino,
At the end of the night I'm through,
I lay my head on my pillow
And my last thought is of you…

Dove Cry

When you walk into a room,
All of my pain goes away,
I feel my heart strings,
Flutter like a butterfly,
I know you have your dreams,
That I am no part of,
But if you think of me,
When you hear coos of a dove
Know my heart cries for you,
With great sadness in the air,
And no matter what you do,
No one else could ever compare…

Angels Down The Hall

Send in the clowns,
My babies gone to sleep,
I need some happy faces,
I've gotten in too deep,
Take me by the hand,
There's angels down the hall,
I promise not to cry,
I promise not to fall,
Carry out my suitcase,
I won't be coming back,
I know you won't be sorry,
Cause Heaven's got your back…

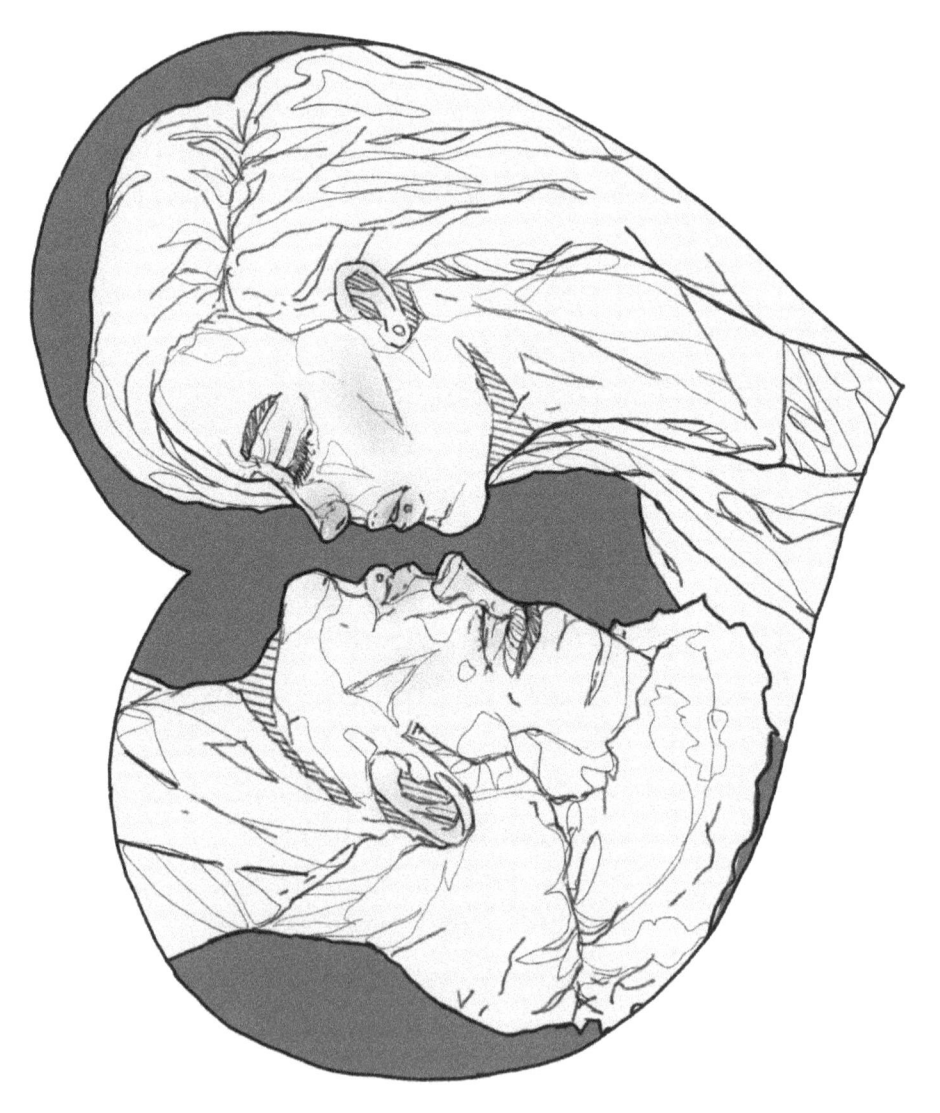

Love

Love is a powerful emotion,
It can take grown Man to his knees,
It can wake him in the middle of the night,
All alone between the sheets,
It can make him run for miles,
Find him no matter where he goes,
It can stop him from growing old,
Tell a truth that no ones told,
Love can make him happy,
It can also make him sad,
And if he never shares it,
It can also drive him mad…

The Sweater

A strong man working,
Extreme energy,
Deep voice assuring who worked beside him,
Tight fitted sweater,
holding every muscle in it's perfect place.
Theatrical comedy bursting from his lips,
Astonished by his knowledge and perfection of words,
I chose to watch him from a distance,
Like going to a play at a theatre,
He was a light that climbed softly onto the stage,
Shinning into my corner,
Where the texture of his hand reaches out,
Ever so gently to touch my soul…

Poppa Zeno

Poppa Zeno I love the way you cradle,
My Mother in your arms,
And how you make your children
Feel just like treasured charms,
And the time you took each day,
To teach me how to pray,
I love the way you act so strong,
Like nothings ever wrong,
How you always seem to light the way,
Through all your darkest days,
If only you could laugh out loud,
Grab your baseball bat and glove,
Take us out to the ball game,
Where my Mother fell in love…

Filly

I heard a noise,
Late last night,
Coming from the barn,
Sounded like a kicking horse,
Had casted upon the wall,
There laying helplessly,
Upon the barns stall floor,
A tiny little filly,
Crept up to its stall door,
Everyone tried to help her nurse,
While her Mother bit and kicked,
Soon they rested quietly,
As visitors came and went...

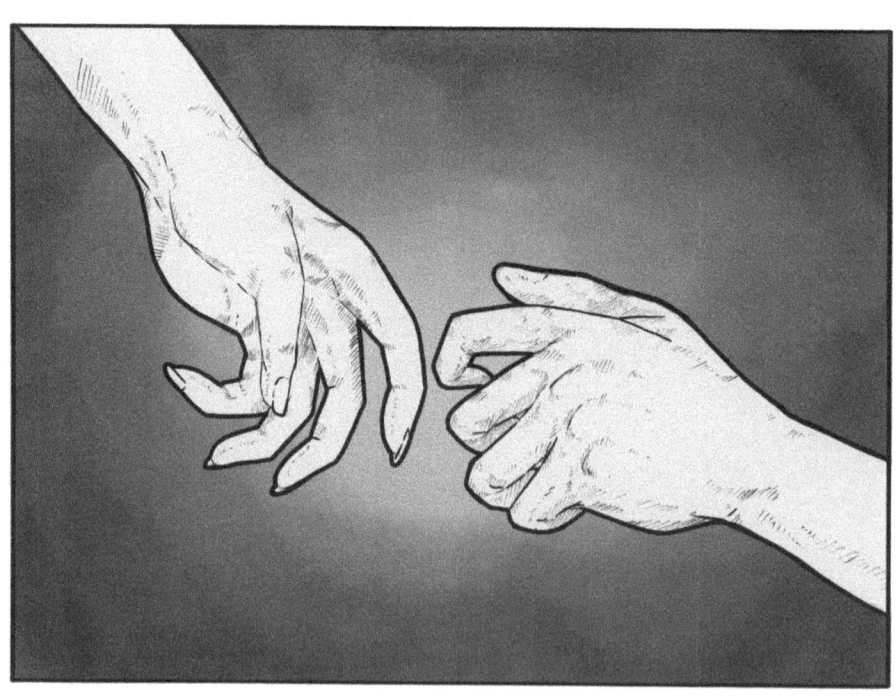

His Truth

She trusted his smile,
And walked alongside his truth,
As his soul poured onto her lap,
She had a choice to listen,
Or to walk away,
She didn't have enough trust to stay,
He invited her to seize the day,
She had the time and chose to play,
He talked as though he wanted to die,
She prayed alongside her faith and cried,
He spoke his truths,
But she didn't understand,
Now it's too late,
He dealt her a new hand,
Time was ticking,
He passed her by,
That alone shows he will lie,
She hit the exit button,
And she walked away,
Now he can live his truth,
And she's gonna be okay...

Masters of Destruction

Masters of Destruction,
Wake the Zombies from the street,
To carry out their orders,
To take a stand,
Or take a seat,
Masters of Destruction,
The World's about to change,
What our fathers always told us,
Keep your enemies close at range,
Masters of Destruction,
Wake the Zombies from the street,
To carry out their orders,
To take a stand,
Or take a seat,
From the backs of Immigration,
We kept our youth from ball and chains.
We fought to make life better,
And to make our freedom rain.

℘

Era of Time

I know we are from different
era's of time,
You have your dreams,
And I have mine.
The warmth of your hug,
The gentle caress of your hand,
Makes me wish
You were my Man,
But you live inside a dream,
Too far for me to reach,
So until we meet again
I will learn to understand...

The Edge

Sitting quietly on the edge
Just outside the wall
your voice so calm
While you stand so tall
Waiting for the light
The moon shines through
Leading the way
From me to you
How did we get here
I was lost in the dark
Then you found me
I saw your spark...

www.ingramcontent.com/pod-product-compliance
Lightning Source LLC
Chambersburg PA
CBHW051555120626
46551CB00013B/1525